JAN 2 5 1996	DATE DUE	
FEB 0 1 1996		
APR 4 - 1996		
SEP 1 9 1996		
AUG ? 2002		
NOV 0 4 2002		

THE HOLOCAUST

THE HISTORY OF A HATRED

Stuart A. Kallen

Published by Abdo & Daughters, 4940 Viking Drive, Suite 622, Edina, Minnesota 55435.

Library bound edition distributed by Rockbottom Books, Pentagon Tower, P.O. Box 36036, Minneapolis, Minnesota 55435.

Printed in the United States.

Cover Photo credit: Bettmann Archives
Interior Photo credits: Wide World photos, page 5
                   Archive photos, pages 6, 14, 19, 24, 27
                   Bettmann Archives, pages 10, 12, 16, 21, 23, 25
Map created by John Hamilton

Edited By Rosemary Wallner

Kallen, Stuart A., 1955-
    The History of a Hatred / by Stuart A. Kallen.
        p.   cm. -- (The Holocaust)
    Includes bibliography and index.
    ISBN 1-56239-350-2
    1. Antisemitism--History--Juvenile literature.
    [1.Antisemitism.]   I. Title.   II. Series: Holocaust (Edina, Minn.)
    DS145.K325 1994
    305.8'924--dc20   94-17820
                                            CIP
                                            AC

Table of Contents

Foreword

The Holocaust is a tragic time in world history. It was a time of prejudice and bias turned to hate and the persecution of an ethnic group by persons who came into a position of power, allowing them to carry out that hate.

The Holocaust series depicts what prejudice and biases can lead to; how men, women and children—simply because they were Jewish—died horrible deaths.

When a child is born it has no prejudices. Bias must be learned and someone has to display it.

The goal of this series is to enlighten children and help them recognize the ignorance of prejudice so that future generations will be tolerant, understanding, compassionate, and free of prejudice.

Acknowledgments:

Rabbi Morris Allen
        Beth Jacob Congregation

Dr. Stewart Ross
        Mankato State University

Special Thanks to The United States Holocaust Memorial Museum

CHAPTER ONE

THE HISTORY
OF HATRED

*T*he dictionary defines the word holocaust as "complete destruction, devastation, especially by fire." Today that word is most often used, with a capital "H," to refer to a dark period in human history when one nation—Nazi Germany—and its leader—Adolf Hitler—tried to murder every Jewish person in Europe.

From 1933 to 1945, the Nazis killed six million Jewish men, women, and children in factory death camps. This number was two-thirds of all the Jews in Europe. Tens of millions of other innocent victims also died. Gypsies, homosexuals, people who were physically and mentally disabled, and anyone who opposed the Nazis were sent to death camps. But as a survivor of the nightmare, writer Elie Wiesel said, "Not all victims were Jewish, but all Jews were victims."

Elie Wiesel, survivor of the Nazi Holocaust, is the chairman of the U.S. Holocaust Memorial Council.

Usually when mass groups of people are murdered during a war it is because their government holds power or land that the murderers want. But to Hitler, the Jews were to be destroyed because they were, as he said, "vermin, snakes, and parasites." The Nazis would not be satisfied until each and every Jew on the face of the Earth was annihilated.

How could such an event take place? Why did the Nazis think that they could murder all the Jews and get away with it? How could the rest of the world stand by and give Hitler free reign to pursue his twisted goals?

To understand the answers to these questions, we must go back thousands of years—back to the time of Christ and beyond. That's because the seeds of Hitler's evil dream were planted long ago and far away. And his loathing of the Jews was nothing new. He only brought to reality what had been a long, dark history of hatred.

Adolf Hitler, the head of the Nazi Party in Germany. His goal was to conquer Europe and annihilate every Jewish person on Earth.

CHAPTER TWO

TO THE LAND WHERE THE MILK AND HONEY FLOWED

*T*raditional Jewish thought holds that the Jewish people can trace their ancestry back more than 4,000 years to Abraham, the first Jew. He and his descendants were known as Hebrews until the time of Jacob. Jacob was given the name Israel. Jacob's descendants were known as Israelites. When the kingdom of Judah was formed in Palestine, its people were given the name Judeans, or Jews. No matter where the people of Judah traveled, they thought of themselves as Judeans or Jews. Since that time, the words Israelite, Hebrew, or Jew have been used to describe the Jewish people.

Palestine was a tiny country of 10,000 square miles—about the size of the U. S. state of Vermont. Yet it always played an important role in world history, as it still does in the twentieth century. That is because Palestine sits between three continents—Africa, Asia, and Europe. Down through time, many great nations sent their armies through the narrow, coastal plain of Palestine to invade other countries. The Egyptians, Assyrians, Babylonians, Greeks, and Romans have all, at one time, ruled that land.

Throughout the centuries, the footprints of marching armies left many paths of destruction through Palestine. Many of the people who lived there, including the Jews, developed a hatred of war and the horrors it brings. With the hatred of war came a passion for peace and justice.

ISRAEL

Acre
Haifa

Sea
of
Galilee

Ramat Gan
Tel Aviv-Yafo
Holon

West
Bank

River Jordan

Jerusalem

Bethlehem
Hebron

Gaza

Dead Sea

(Hatch marks
indicate areas
occupied by
Israel)

Be 'er Sheva

Negev
Desert

Elat

100 miles

The Middle East

2,500 miles

But Palestine was more than a war zone. It was also a major trade route between great continents. Caravans laden with gold, spices, cloth, and merchandise crossed through the area.

In ancient times, Palestine was a rich and fertile land. In fact, the Bible calls it the "land of milk and honey." Wheat, barley, figs, pomegranates, olives, and honey fed the people who called this land their home.

Because Palestine was such a wonderful place, many tribes of people blossomed there. Beside the Jews, there were Canaanites, Hittites, Phoenicians, Philistines, and others. Each tribe had its own king and its own corner of the country. All these people spoke a similar language and had a common religion and culture. Those people and their culture were called Semitic.

As for religion, the people of Palestine were idol worshipers. They believed in dozens of gods and goddesses. They had major and minor deities that they worshiped with ceremonies and animal sacrifices. There were hundreds of ceremonies involving life, death, the universe, and the nature of the human soul.

The Israelites began to believe that there was only one God. This One God was a Supreme Being who expected people's lives to be hallowed by their daily practice of the arts of peace and prayer, of social justice and human unity. They believed "When God made the first man, He fashioned him out of the dust that He had gathered from all the countries of the world." This faith in one God set the Israelites apart from other ancient tribes.

Much of traditional Jewish belief can be found in the Old Testament of the Bible. Most of these stories are well-known— how God created the world in six days; how Adam and Eve were tempted in the Garden of Eden; how Noah built his ark and survived the flood. The foundation of Jewish religion is the story of God showing himself to Moses and giving him the Ten Commandments.

Over the centuries, the Israelites became a great nation. They lived by the Ten Commandments and other laws of ethics and justice. They had great kingdoms under kings David and Solomon. Jerusalem was their capital city and the Temple there was the center of their lives.

The story of Moses and the Ten Commandments from the Old Testament helped to define the Jews as a one deity religion.

CHAPTER THREE

THE MESSIAH

*I*n 63 B.C. Roman soldiers swept into Palestine. Thousands were killed and the Romans forced a new government on the people there. The Romans heavily taxed people and oppressed them without mercy. Some people became very rich as others hovered on the brink of starvation. The Jewish belief in one God brought them into sharp conflict with the Roman rulers who believed in many gods and goddesses.

The daily life of the Jews went on as usual. In the marketplace, Jewish farmers sold fruits and vegetables. Merchants sold fabrics, spice, jewelry, and other wares. Moneylenders, the bankers of the time, lent money to people for a fee.

The Jewish community itself was split into sects. Each one competed for believers. Out of this competition, a new religion arose. The founder of the religion was a Jewish teacher, or rabbi, named Yehoshua, which means "help comes from God" in Hebrew. Yehoshua is Joshua in English, and Jesus in Greek.

Jesus had a group of Jewish followers. From them he chose a group of 12 disciples he called Apostles. He preached in the streets and gathered crowds. He urged people to live simply, help the poor, and feed the hungry. He was critical of the moneylenders in the market who charged high interest rates. One day Jesus went to the stalls of the moneylenders and overturned their tables. Jesus's followers said that he was the son of God—that he was the Messiah. They called him Christ, which means Messiah in Greek.

Such claims were against Jewish belief. In Jewish thinking, only God was divine. God was mysterious, invisible, and possessed no known shape. God could not have children. God could not father a son.

Jesus Christ preached publicly about the Kingdom of God. He opposed Roman rule and his followers called him King. Some considered him the son of God.

But some Jews believed that when the suffering of the people became unbearable, that God, or the Messiah, would return to Earth and save them. Because Roman rule was so harsh, many believed that the Messiah had appeared. Many gave up their traditional Jewish beliefs in hopes of a redeemer who would have the power to bring the enemies of Israel to justice. They believed Jesus Christ to be that Messiah.

Jesus Christ lived and died as a Jew. His mother, Mary, was Jewish. His followers Peter and Paul and the first Apostles were all Jewish.

Jesus preached publicly that the Kingdom of God was at hand. To the Romans this sounded like high treason against the Emperor of Rome. The Romans viewed Jesus as a rabble-rouser. He stirred up the people. Some began calling him King. The Romans arrested Jesus and put him on trial for plotting against the state. He was found guilty and sentenced to death in the usual Roman way, by being nailed to a cross, a crucifixion. Jesus's followers believed that he was the Son of God.

The Gospels were written forty to seventy years after Jesus's death. The writers blamed Jews for the death of Jesus. Jews, however, do not believe that they caused Jesus's death. For one thing, only a Roman governor could order an execution. And Jesus was a practicing Jew. Jesus did not seek to create a new religion. He only wanted to liberalize Jewish law. He posed no threat to the Jews. Over one million Jews lived in Palestine and Jesus only had about 250 followers when he died.

Yet the blame for Jesus's death would hang like a sword over the heads of Jews for almost 2,000 years.

CHAPTER FOUR

THE WANDERING JEWS

*M*ost Jews did not believe that Jesus was the next Messiah. Many were afraid that the Roman wrath against Jesus would be taken out on all the Jews. Many Jews who were working for the Romans supported the government of Rome in order to protect themselves. Some Jews were corrupt and supported Rome's harsh policies. Like any modern city, there were people with a wide range of beliefs and loyalties.

The Romans used this division among the Jews to divide the tribe and conquer. They found it politically useful to blame the death of Jesus on the Jews.

In A.D. 70 the Jews led a revolt to try to overthrow the Roman rule. Over one million Jews were killed in a war that lasted three years. The Romans destroyed the Jewish Temple and razed Jerusalem to the ground.

This is a collage of a Roman soldier.

Rome forced the remaining Jews out of Jerusalem and forbade them from ever returning.

The Jews were now homeless, wandering the Earth in search of a place where they would not be oppressed. With them they carried the Christian blame for killing Jesus. Jews became a mistrusted minority the world over.

After the Jewish Revolt, the blame for Jesus's death took on a life of its own. When the Gospels were written, Saint Paul wrote phrases such as, "The Jews who killed the Lord Jesus..." and "The Jews who are heedless of God's will and their fellow man...." Some Christians used these words to justify hatred of the Jews, called anti-Semitism. Jewish historians believe that the Roman persecution of the Christians caused the authors of the Gospels to write as they did. The Christians feared Rome and so portrayed the Romans in a good light and the Jews in a bad light.

The followers of Jesus were called Jewish Christians. At first, only Jews were disciples of Christ. But soon the Christians began to admit pagans, Greeks, Romans, and others into their circle of believers. The Jews became outnumbered. Soon all followers of Jesus were simply called Christians.

Four hundred years after Jesus died, in the fourth century, Christianity became the official religion of the Roman Empire. The Roman Catholic Church was born. Church fathers condemned the Jews as an accursed people, rejected by God. They said that all Jews should be blamed for the death of Jesus forever. They forbade Christians to marry Jews. Conversion to Judaism was punishable by death.

Outside the church, Jews lived in fragile harmony with their neighbors. They were respected as shopkeepers, doctors, and international traders.

This changed in 1095 when Pope Urban II launched a Christian Crusade against the Jews and Muslims. By then the Jews had moved back to Jerusalem. Urban II urged the Christian princes to win back Jerusalem from the Jewish and Muslim "infidels." The Christian Crusade unleashed the worst calamity that the Jews had ever known. In 1096, marauding mobs destroyed Jewish communities in northern France and throughout Germany and Bohemia. When the crusaders arrived in Jerusalem, they locked all the Jews in the Temple and burned it down. An eyewitness wrote, "Men rode in blood up to their knees. It was a just and splendid judgment by God that this place should be filled with the blood of the unbelievers." All the Muslims were slain in a similar manner.

When Richard the Lionhearted was crowned King of England in 1189, Jews were massacred throughout the country.

Pope Urban II bidding farewell to the crusaders as they prepare to Christianize the Muslim and Jewish world. The Crusades took place 1,000 years after Christ died. Notice the crucifixes next to Pope Urban.

CHAPTER FIVE

MYTHS, LIES, AND MARTIN LUTHER

*I*n 1215 Pope Innocent III decreed that the Jews must wear yellow badges to mark themselves. At Easter, the clergy told people to throw stones at Jews as punishment for failing to accept Christ as God. In some countries Jews were forced to wear special, pointed hats.

As the hatred continued, myths sprang up about Jewish religious practices. One myth was that Jews used the blood of Christian children to make matzo (unleavened bread) for their Passover dinner. Other myths followed. Some said that the Jews poisoned the wells of Christians to kill them. Mobs excited by these wild stories fell upon the nearest community of Jews and murdered them. Local priests did nothing to stop them. For hundreds of years, politicians used the myths and lies about Jews to stir up peasants in the countryside. As the superstitions continued, Christians separated Jesus from his Jewish roots.

Throughout the centuries, some popes and archbishops tried to stop the killings. They said that, because of Jewish religious teachings, the Jews were not allowed to mistreat anyone. But people did not listen to the words of the holy men. Attacks against Jews continued. Usually, the mob divided up the property of the Jews and the competition from the Jews in business was eliminated.

Jews were forbidden to own land and to practice most trades. With no other way to earn a living, many turned to banking and money lending to survive. This, too, would haunt the Jews for centuries.

By the late Middle Ages, the Jews, a powerless minority in every land, had become objects of hatred and persecution all over Europe.

In Spain, Jews had once been left alone to prosper and grow. But in 1492, the same year Columbus set sail for the New World, 100,000 Jews were expelled from Spain. Those who remained were tortured in hideous ways.

In Italy and Germany, Jews were openly repressed and separated into certain neighborhoods, called ghettos. Their holy books were burned. In the artwork of the period, Jews were portrayed as devils in human form. In the minds of the common people, the Jews were associated with Satan, devil worship, the black arts, and everything negative. They were called the "children of the Devil." Some peasants, who had never seen a Jew, thought all Jews had horns.

In 1519, a German, Martin Luther, rebelled against the Roman Catholic Church and established the Protestant faith. In 1543, Luther wrote a 90-page book called "On the Jews and Their Lies." Luther wrote:

> They have been blood-thirsty bloodhounds and murderers of all Christendom for more than fourteen hundred years... We are at fault for not slaying them. Rather, we allow them to live freely in our midst despite all their murdering, cursing, blaspheming, lying, and defaming. I shall give you my sincere advice...to set fire to their synagogues or

schools...their houses also be razed and destroyed...all their prayer books and Talmudic writings, in which such idolatry, lies, cursing, and blasphemy are taught, be taken from them...their rabbis be forbidden to teach henceforth on pain of loss of life and limb...safe conduct on the highways be abolished completely for the Jews...all cash and treasure of silver and gold be taken from them and put aside for safekeeping.

Martin Luther proposed that Jews be forced into camps and used as slave labor until they became just like the Christians, or assimilated. Four hundred years later, Hitler and the Nazis used the words of Martin Luther as an excuse to put the Jews in concentration camps and kill them.

Martin Luther broke away from the Roman Catholic Church to establish the Protestant faith. His anti-semetic writings were used by the Nazis to persecute the Jews 400 years after he lived.

CHAPTER SIX

THE PROTOCOLS OF THE ELDERS OF ZION

*B*y the nineteenth century, the church had become less powerful in Europe. Jews had slowly become one with the rest of European society, culture, and politics. Many Jews had become journalists, publishers, teachers, bankers, and other members of upper-class society. In a few hundred years, many Jews had gone from being peasants to joining the peak of European high society. No other group among Europeans had made such a leap in so short a time. This created jealousy and resentment among the poor and working-class Europeans.

In Germany in 1860, a writer, Sir John Retcliffe, wrote a novel titled *To Sedan*. One chapter dealt with twelve Jewish elders who gathered in a cemetery at midnight to make plans with the devil to take over the world. Although the book was fiction—anti-Semites seized it and rewrote it to make it look like fact. The twelve elders were replaced with one rabbi. The rabbi spoke not at a cemetery but at a secret society. The society plotted to take over the world. The rewritten book became *The Rabbi's Speech* and was published all over Europe, including Russia.

In Russia, the secret police of Czar Nicholas II put together a pamphlet using *The Rabbi's Speech* and other works. They titled it *The Protocols of the Elders of Zion*. The pamphlet was written to scare people about the Jews.

At the turn of the 19th century, Czar Nicholas II of Russia
professed hatred toward Jews.

The secret police claimed that the document that they had written was actually written by Jews. *The Protocols* repeated all the myths and lies that had been said about Jews for hundreds of years, including the myth that Jews drank children's blood and planned to take over the world.

Czar Nicholas realized that *The Protocols* was a fake. But his secret police published the document and it spread throughout Europe. In Russia, the document was used to organize pogroms (attacks) on Jewish communities. In 1881 and 1882 peasants shouted "Kill the Jews and save Russia" while they massacred Jews. In 1903 Russians savagely murdered Jews during the Jewish holiday of Passover. They mutilated Jews and looted 1,500 Jewish homes and stores.

In the 1920s Henry Ford, president of the Ford Motor Company, published *The Protocols* in the newspapers he owned. Ford believed all those myths about Jews. When Jews protested, Ford apologized. Today, *The Protocols of the Elders of Zion* is still widely published in Saudi Arabia, Iran, Iraq, and among other anti-Semitic groups the world over.

CHAPTER SEVEN

THE RISE OF THE NAZIS

*B*y the late nineteenth and early twentieth century, European Jews had risen to many important positions. Albert Einstein was a scientist. Franz Kafka was a writer. Gustav Mahler was a composer. Sigmund Freud founded the study of psychology. Along with many others, the work of these Jews deeply changed European civilization.

Psychologist Sigmund Freud.

Scientist Albert Einstein.

These successes created a new wave of anti-Semitism. In Germany, the loss of World War I gave rise to a new political party, the Nazis. The Nazis, and their leader Adolf Hitler, blamed the Jews for the collapse of the German economy. They revived the myths and lies about Jews that had been circulating for centuries. They used radio and rallies to spread their message of hatred against the Jews.

Adolf Hitler and the Nazi party took over Germany when the country was vulnerable. The economy was sagging and the people were looking for a new leader. Hitler offered a renewal based on hate and violence.

The Nazis dug up a false nineteenth-century theory of human racial history. The theory placed the Germans and Austrians, called Aryans, at the top of the human family tree. It placed the Africans at the bottom and the Asians in between. A separate category was created for Arabs and Jews, or Semitics. This theory, created in 1879, used so-called scientific thinking to justify hatred of the Jews.

One of the believers of this theory was the famous German composer Richard Wagner (1813-1883). Obsessed with ethnic purity, Wagner wrote racist and anti-Semitic pamphlets. Forty years later Hitler embraced Wagner's theories as well as his music.

Hitler, who believed in the purity of the German race, never hid his intentions toward the Jews. In speech after speech, Hitler called for the annihilation of all European Jewry. By 1942, his words had become reality.

Richard Wagner (1813-1883), German composer who wrote anti-Semitic pamphlets.

CHAPTER EIGHT

THE DISTANCE NARROWS

*I*t took almost 2,000 years for the official Catholic Church to declare the Jews innocent for the death of Jesus. In October 1965 the Second Vatican Council issued a document, "In Our Age." It said that the crucifixion could not be blamed on the Jews living then or now. Rome regretted deeply the persecution, prejudice, and hatred of the Jews. But the document did not mention the Holocaust or Christianity's long history of anti-Semitism. It also called the Church the "new people of God," and mentioned that Jews could be faulted for rejecting the Gospel. The gulf between Rome and the Jews remained.

In January 1994, Pope John Paul thawed relations with the Jews when he began diplomatic relations with the nation of Israel. Now, the Roman Catholic Church has accepted Israel's right to exist. After centuries of ill will and misunderstanding, two of the great religions of the world have begun to come together to live in peace.

Pope John Paul, head of the Roman Catholic Church, began diplomatic relations with the nation of Israel in 1994.

GLOSSARY

A. D. - abbreviation of the Latin words *ano Domini*, meaning "in the year of our Lord." Used with dates to define period of time after the death of Christ.

Annihilate - to reduce to complete ruin, to wipe out completely.

Anti-Semitism - hatred of Jews.

Apostle - one of the twelve disciples of Christ sent out to preach the Gospel.

Assimilate - to become one with or absorb into. When the Jews became assimilated, they took up the manners and customs of another country or people.

B. C. - before Christ. Used with dates to define the period of time before the birth of Christ.

Blasphemy - profanity, cursing.

Concentration camp - a guarded camp for the detention and forced labor of political prisoners.

Crucifixion - to nail someone to a cross so that they die.

Crusades - military campaigns that Christians undertook in the eleventh, twelfth, and thirteenth centuries. The purpose of the Crusades was to regain the Holy Land and kill non-Christians.

Deities - gods and goddesses.

Descendant - a person who is related to an ancestor.

Disciple - a follower of Christ.

Divine - god-like.

Ghetto - a section of a city in most European countries where all Jews were forced to live.

Hallowed - holy, sacred.

Holocaust - the mass extermination of Jews in Nazi Germany.

Infidel - a person who does not accept the faith of Christianity or Islam.

Matzo - flat, cracker-like bread that Jewish people eat during the holiday of Passover.

Messiah - the promised and expected deliverer of the Jewish people. Also, Jesus Christ.

Myth - a false story or tale.

New Testament - a portion of the Bible recording the experiences of Christ.

Old Testament - the complete Bible of the Jews.

Palestine - a territory on the East Coast of the Mediterranean Sea that was occupied by the Hebrews in Biblical times.

Passover - A Jewish holiday celebrating the deliverance of the Hebrews from slavery in ancient Egypt.

Persecution - to be harassed with harsh treatment because of one's race, religion, or beliefs.

Pogrom - an organized massacre of Jews in Russia.

Prejudice - hatred or dislike of someone because of their race, religion, or beliefs.

Protocol - an original draft of a document.

Racist - a person who believes that their race is superior to others.

Redeemer - one who sets free or saves another.

Repress - to keep under control or stifle another person.

Semite - a member of any of a various ancient and modern people, especially Hebrews or Arabs.

Ten Commandments - the ten laws of conduct God gave Moses. Jewish tradition is based on the Ten Commandments.

BIBLIOGRAPHY

Adler, David A. *We Remember the Holocaust.* New York: Henry Holt and Company, 1989.

Aharoni, Yohanan, and Avi-Yonah, Michael. *The Macmillan Bible Atlas.* New York: Macmillan, 1993.

Ausubel, Nathan, and Gross, David C. *Pictorial History of the Jewish People.* New York: Crown Publishers, Inc., 1953, 1984.

Berenbaum, Michael. *The World Must Know.* Boston: Little, Brown and Company, 1993.

Block, Gay, and Drucker. *Malka Rescuers.* New York: Holmes & Meier Publications, Inc., 1992

Chaikin, Miriam A. *Nightmare in History: The Holocaust 1933-1945.* New York: Clarion Books, 1987.

Dawidowicz, Lucy S. *The War Against the Jews 1933-1945.* New York: Seth Press, 1986.

Flannery, Edward H. *The Anguish of the Jews.* New York: Paulist Press, 1985.

Gilbert, Martin. *Final Journey.* New York: Mayflower Books, 1979.

Gilbert, Martin. *The Macmillan Atlas of the Holocaust.* New York: Macmillan, 1982.

Greenfeld, Howard. *The Hidden Children.* New York: Ticknor & Fields, 1993.

Landau, Elaine. *The Warsaw Ghetto Uprising.* New York: New Discovery Books, 1992.

Paldiel, Mordecai. *The Path of the Righteous.* Hoboken, New Jersey: KTAV Publishing House, Inc., 1993.

Index